INTELLECTUAL
PILGRIMS

Also by Edwin J. Feulner, Jr.

The March of Freedom: Modern Classics in Conservative Thought, 1998

Conservatives Stalk the House: The Story of the Republican Study Committee, 1983

Looking Back, 1981

Congress and the New International Economic Order, 1976

China—The Turning Point, editor, 1976

Trading with the Communists, with Samuel F. Clabaugh, 1968

INTELLECTUAL PILGRIMS

The Fiftieth
Anniversary of the
Mont Pelerin Society

EDWIN J. FEULNER, JR.

Edwin J. Feulner, Jr.
214 Massachusetts Avenue, N.E.
Washington, D.C. 20002
1-202-546-4400

In Memory Of

MAX THURN

Maximilian Graf Thurn-Valsassina (1911–1991),
Secretary of The Mont Pelerin Society (1976–1988),
Colleague, Counselor, and Friend.

TABLE OF CONTENTS

ACKNOWLEDGMENTS

During my tenure as President of The Mont Pelerin Society, I relied on my predecessors for both their inspiration and their continuing counsel. My inspiration from the Society's founder and first President, Friedrich von Hayek, has been commemorated in *The Wall Street Journal* on the occasion of the 100th anniversary of his birth (in the May 7, 1999, issue).

The Society's past Presidents—Wilhelm Roepke, Friedrich Lutz, Milton Friedman, Arthur Shenfield, Gaston Leduc, George Stigler, Manuel Ayau, Chiaki Nishiyama, Ralph Harris, James Buchanan, Herbert Giersch, Antonio Martino, Gary Becker, Max Hartwell, and Pascal Salin—have been counselors and, in many cases, close personal friends to me over the years.

The Mont Pelerin Society's current officers, Secretary Carl-Johan Westholm and Treasurer Leonard Liggio, and my distinguished successor as President, Ramon Diaz, all shared their insights with me.

The Secretary of The Philadelphia Society and long-time Mont Pelerin Society member, Bill Campbell, Mont Pelerin colleagues Michael Novak, Robert Sirico, and Bill and Mary Peterson have given me continuing friendly counsel on this project.

Bridgett Wagner, Phil Truluck, Stuart Butler, Jerry O'Driscoll, and Henry Manne constantly prodded me to improve the quality of this volume. In addition, I owe particular thanks to my colleague and friend, Joe Shattan, for his editorial assistance. My immediate staff, including Jennifer Donaldson, Jessica Zigmond, and Viktoria Ziebarth, were helpful in its preparation. To all of them I am grateful.

Any faults in either the analysis or the prescriptions are my own.

Edwin J. Feulner, Jr.
July 1999

STATEMENT OF AIMS
MONT PELERIN
SOCIETY

ADOPTED APRIL 8, 1947

A group of economists, historians, philosophers and other students of public affairs from Europe and the United States met at Mont Pelerin, Switzerland, from April 1st to 10th, 1947, to discuss the crisis of our times. This group, being desirous of perpetuating its existence for promoting further intercourse and for inviting the collaboration of other like-minded persons has agreed upon the following statement of aims.

The central values of civilization are in danger. Over large stretches of the earth's surface the essential conditions of human dignity and freedom have already disappeared. In others they are under constant menace from the development of current tendencies of policy. The position of the individual and the voluntary group are progressively undermined by extensions of arbitrary power. Even that most precious possession of Western Man, freedom of thought and expression, is threatened by the spread of creeds which, claiming the privilege of tolerance when in the position of a minority, seek only to establish a position of power in which they can suppress and obliterate all views but their own.

The group holds that these developments have been fostered by the growth of a view of history which denies all absolute moral standards and by the growth of theories which question the desirability of the rule of law. It holds further that they have been fostered by a decline of belief in private property and the competitive market; for without the diffused power and initiative associated with these institutions it is difficult to imagine a society in which freedom may be effectively preserved.

Believing that what is essentially an ideological movement must be met by intellectual argument and the reassertion of valid ideals, the group having made a preliminary exploration of the ground, is of the opinion the further study is desirable inter alia in regard to the following matters:

1. The analysis and explanation of the nature of the present crisis so as to bring home to others its essential moral and economic origins. ·

2. The redefinition of the functions of the state so as to distinguish more clearly between the totalitarian and liberal order.

3. Methods of re-establishing the rule of law and of assuring its development in such manner that individuals and groups are not in a position to encroach upon the freedom of others and private rights are not allowed to become a basis of predatory power.

4. The possibility of establishing minimum standards by means not inimical to initiative and the functioning of the market.

5. Methods of combating the misuse of history for the furtherance of creeds hostile to liberty.

6. The problem of the creation of an international order conducive to the safeguarding of peace and liberty and permitting the establishment of harmonious international economic relations.

The group does not aspire to conduct propaganda. It seeks to establish no meticulous and hampering orthodoxy. It aligns itself with no particular party. Its object is solely, by facilitating the exchange of views among minds inspired by certain ideals and broad conceptions held in common, to contribute to the preservation and improvement of the free society.

Mont Pelerin (Vaud), Switzerland,
April 8, 1947.

INTRODUCTION

*D*r. Johnson undoubtedly was correct when he told James Boswell, back in 1777, that "when a man knows he is to be hanged in a fortnight, it concentrates his mind wonderfully." Next to a public hanging, though, the most mind-concentrating event I know of is having to deliver a major address on the conservative prospect before the distinguished members of the Mont Pelérin Society. Yet, as the Society's president from 1996 to 1998, it was my daunting duty—as well as my high honor—to address my colleagues not once, but thrice, on this general theme. The three speeches contained in this volume—products of a not-inconsiderable expenditure of "blood, sweat, and tears"—constitute my best effort to think through the problems facing classical liberals today, and to present an updated classical liberal agenda for a post-socialist world.

The Mont Pelerin Society was founded in 1947 by Friedrich von Hayek and 38 other intellects and leaders to uphold the principles of what Europeans call "liberalism" (as opposed to "statism") and what we Americans call "conservatism" (as opposed to "liberalism"): free markets, limited governments, and personal liberty under the rule of law.[1]

Today, the Society's membership, drawn from some 40 countries around the world, has increased more than tenfold.[2] Without exception, these members—Nobel laureates, high government officials, scholars, business leaders, and journalists—are men and women of outstanding ability and genuine attainment. Hence my nervousness at presuming to instruct them on the tasks facing us. Hence, too, my

---

1. Throughout this volume, the word "liberal" is used in the classical European sense—that is, denoting a believer in liberty. (See F. A. von Hayek, *The Constitution of Liberty,* Chapter XI, "Why I Am Not a Conservative.")

2. The history of the Mont Pelerin Society as told by Professor Max Hartwell, *A History of the Mont Pelerin Society* (Indianapolis, Ind.: Liberty Fund, 1995). Professor Hartwell was the President of the Mont Pelerin Society from 1992 to 1994.

relief at the warm reception my remarks received, and my hope that they may prove of some interest to a wider audience as well.

When the Mont Pelerin Society was formed more than 50 years ago, socialism—in both its "hard" Leninist and "soft" social democratic variants—was everywhere in the ascendant. This explains the reason Hayek and his colleagues regarded themselves as an embattled minority desperately struggling to stave off the impending darkness. By contrast, today socialism has been decisively discredited, while the anti-statist views of Mont Pelerin's founders have been triumphantly vindicated. But if virtually everyone professes to acknowledge the failures and shortcomings of Leviathan, what tasks face the Mont Pelerin Society—and the classical liberal movement as a whole—now? In one form or another, all three speeches in this volume revolve around this crucial issue of self-definition.

A related theme, also running through these speeches, has to do with the relationship between *politico sensu largo*—"politics in the large sense" of waging the battle of ideas in order to establish the nature of the common good—and *politico sensu stricto*—"politics in the narrow sense" of deciding who shall govern.

Like many classical liberals, I used to think that politics in the narrow sense was merely a function of politics in the larger sense: Once the intellectual battle was over, and the common good was rightly understood, political candidates with the wrong ideas would find it impossible to get (re)elected, and politicians with the right ideas would be swept into office, where they would proceed to dismantle the welfare state and reaffirm the traditional classical liberal principles of limited government and liberty under the law.

In my view, recent events demonstrate conclusively that this understanding of the relationship between politics in the large and narrow senses is flawed. We have won the battle of ideas. Everyone, even dyed-in-the-wool statists like Bill Clinton, now agrees that the "era of big government" is over. Yet big government continues to grow ever bigger. The thick, heavy bureaucracies of yesteryear are still in place; indeed, they are thicker and heavier than ever.

Classical liberalism's manifest inability to translate its intellectual victories into political victories that seriously roll back the size and power of the socialist welfare state demonstrates that winning the battle of ideas is not enough. For the United States, and for the rest of the world, to climb down successfully from the icy peaks of statism, much more will have to be done—and, in the following speeches, I try to spell out what that "much more" is.

Finally, having to address my Mont Pelerin Society colleagues on the future of our movement forced me to clarify my own classical liberal values. It also forced me to develop, with some degree of concreteness, my vision of what life in a post-welfare state America would be like. In these remarks, I contend that such an America would be more compassionate as well as more efficient; more just as well as more affluent; and more in keeping with the true requirements of human nature than a "nanny state" that undoes the social fabric even as it seeks to stifle human initiative and creativity. As I reflected on it, I determined this vision is both Hayekian and universal. As Professor Janus Beorkman points out, this social role undergirds much of Hayek's thought. And it can be universal rather than strictly North American.

In speeches and meetings with conservatives around the United States—and around the world—the two questions I am asked most frequently are, "If we classical liberals have won, why don't I feel like a winner?" and "If everyone finally agrees with us that big government does more harm than good, shouldn't we now turn our attention to other issues?" The arguments I develop in this slim volume try to answer these questions.

Because my colleagues and I at The Heritage Foundation believe these arguments merit a broad hearing—and because we further believe that the history of the Mont Pelerin Society is a grand and inspiring tale that deserves to become better-known—we decided to make these presidential addresses available to the general public. We hope they will help to reawaken a once vivid, but now all-too-dormant, sense "of the power, ingenuity, and creativity of civil society," as well as to illuminate what I regard to be the main tasks facing American conservatives today: rolling back the social welfare state and building an America in which freedom, opportunity, and civil society flourish.

Edwin J. Feulner, Jr.
Washington, D.C.
July 1999

1

WE ARE ALL LIBERALS NOW— OR ARE WE?

*I*t is a singular honor for me to serve as president of the Mont Pelerin Society. I regard this group, quite simply, as the most distinguished assembly of minds on the face of the planet. Seven of our members—Hayek, Friedman, Stigler, Buchanan, Allais, Coase, and Becker—have received the Nobel Prize for Economics. Others will undoubtedly be Nobel laureates in the future. But of this I am sure:

Presidential Address delivered to the 1997 Special Gathering of the Mont Pelerin Society, April 12, 1997, in Mont Pelerin, Switzerland.

Whoever becomes our Society's eighth Nobel Prize winner, it won't be me!

We are gathered together to celebrate the 50th anniversary of the founding of the Mont Pelerin Society. For organizations, as for individuals, it is no minor event to turn 50. And so, in my remarks this evening, and also in the addresses I intend to deliver in September 1997 at our Barcelona regional meeting and in September 1998 at our Washington, D.C., General Meeting, I want to exercise my prerogative as president to think out loud about us: where we have been, what we have done, and how we might proceed.

It is customary to speak of Mont Pelerin as a society but that, I fear, is already a distortion of reality. Most societies, after all, have a steady address; we have none. Most societies hunger for publicity; we shun it. Most societies have a distinct "party line"; we make a point of welcoming diversity. Our permanent abode, as Max Hartwell has said, is in the "minds and affections" of our members. Our permanent point-of-view is an openness to all points of view that embrace freedom. Our permanent preoccupation is to work out, insofar as we can, a durable philosophy of freedom.

"The immediate purpose of this conference," Friedrich von Hayek said at the opening meeting of the Society in 1947,

> is to provide an opportunity for a comparatively small group of those who in different parts of the world are striving for the same ideals, to get personally acquainted, to profit from one another's experience, and perhaps also to give mutual encouragement.

The reason the 39 men and women who founded the Mont Pelerin Society were in need of "mutual encouragement" was that, in 1947, those who upheld the principles of classical liberalism were a distinct minority. The liberalism that was 19th-century Europe's crowning glory seemed hopelessly discredited by World Wars I and II, by Nazism, and by Stalinism. In the aftermath of these terrible cataclysms no serious person, it was widely thought, could possibly believe in a beneficent social order spontaneously generated by the uncoordinated actions of countless ordinary men and women. Collectivism was the order of the day and socialism, in one form or another, was the wave of the future in the West as well as the East. Leviathan had triumphed.

In trying to envisage how Hayek and the other founder-members of the Mont Pelerin Society must have felt in 1947, I am irresistibly drawn to the biblical image of the Saving Remnant, and to an essay called "Isaiah's Job," written by the distinguished American thinker, Albert Jay Nock. First published in 1936, this witty article tells the story of the Prophet Isaiah, whom God called during the reign of King Uzziah, about 740 B.C., to prophesy to his people. As Nock puts it, the Lord says,

> Tell them what is wrong and why, and what is going to happen unless they have a change of heart and straighten up. Don't mince matters. Make it clear that they are positively down to their last chance. Give it to them good and strong, and keep on giving it to them.

Understandably, Isaiah becomes apprehensive when the Lord adds,

> I suppose I ought to tell you that it won't do any good. The official class and intelligentsia will turn up their noses at you, and the masses will not listen and you will probably be lucky if you get out with your life.

When Isaiah asks why he should bother to prophesy if no one will listen, the Lord replies:

> You do not get the point. There is a Remnant that you know nothing about. They are obscure, unorganized, inarticulate. They need to be encouraged, because when everything has gone completely to the dogs, they are the ones who will come back and build up a new society, and meanwhile your preaching will reassure them and keep them hanging on. Your job is to take care of the Remnant, so be off now and set about it.

Hayek's self-appointed task was the same as Isaiah's—to "take care of the Remnant" and "keep them hanging on"—and founding the Mont Pelerin Society was how he did it. Interestingly, the name Hayek originally chose for our group—the Tocqueville–Acton Society—was rejected by the other members at their founding meeting. "Both Acton and Tocqueville were Catholics and noblemen," noted Professor William Rappard, and this, he felt, might seem unfair to non-Catholics and commoners. "How about the Adam Smith–Tocqueville Society?" asked Professor Aaron Director. "The Periclean Society," suggested

Karl Popper. "The Protagonist Society," said Lionel Robbins. "It is incongruous to name our society after people," offered the ever-helpful Milton Friedman. "We want it to be named after principles."

But if people were incongruous and principles were contentious, there was always the Swiss landscape—and especially its mountains—to fall back on. "How about the Mont Pelerin Society?" asked the Hoover Institution's Professor Karl Brandt. "That is meaningless," Popper shot back. Meaningless or not, however, that was the name the group eventually settled on.

Looking back on that founding meeting half a century ago, it's also worth noting that Hayek did not intend our Society to devote itself exclusively to economic problems. "It is a matter of great regret to me," he said,

> that largely as a result of my personal shortcomings, the membership of the present conference is somewhat unevenly balanced and that historians and political philosophers, instead of being as strongly represented as the economists, are a comparatively small minority.

This imbalance in our membership has never been rectified and may account for the fact that, while we have brilliantly succeeded in developing a critique of, and alternative to, economic interventionism, Hayek's goal of formulating a comprehensive "philosophy of freedom" continues to challenge us.

In February 1965, as a Richard Weaver Fellow at the London School of Economics, I had the good fortune to meet Hayek when he came to deliver a guest lecture. On that occasion, a group of us enjoyed a coffee with him, and we even dared to suggest that we start a group to study his works. He graciously suggested a name—the Old Whig Society—and, at that time, I am pleased to report, we adopted it without argument. Under that title it flourished for several years, irritating our intellectual adversaries to the point that they vandalized our publications display and stole our cash box. (We never discovered whether this was dictated by ideological opposition or crass greed, but to this day I believe it had to be ideological because the sum in question—three shillings sixpence—ruled out enlightened self-interest as a motive!)

In 1968, Clarence Philbrook of the University of North Carolina, who was then the Treasurer of the Mont Pelerin Society, invited me to a general meeting of the Society in Aviemore, Scotland, as one of the Society's guests sponsored by the Earhart Foundation. I have been intimately involved with the Society's affairs ever since. The first meeting of the Society that I attended as a full-fledged member was down this mountain in Montreaux in 1972 and it is still vivid in my memory today, not least because Milton Friedman used the occasion to argue that the battle of economics had been won; our work was done, and we should dissolve the Society. I was quite taken aback by Milton's argument. At home, President Richard Nixon had just imposed wage-and-price controls. Abroad, the Soviet Union was bent on changing the "correlation of forces" while the West fruitlessly pursued a policy of détente. If this is Milton's idea of victory, I asked myself, then I wonder how he would define defeat?

In retrospect, however, it is apparent that what Milton meant when he said that the economic battle had been won was pretty much what Ronald Reagan meant when he said, some years later, that the statists "had had their turn at bat in the 1960s and had struck out." The fundamental flaw of statism—its "fatal conceit," Hayek called it—was its arrogant conviction that policymakers could blithely disregard traditions that embodied the wisdom of generations; that they could impetuously ignore customs whose purposes they didn't understand, and yet they could emerge from the inevitable disasters with their prestige intact and their ideas unchallenged.

So the statists struck out—not just in the United States, but everywhere. Well before the amazing events of the years 1989 to 1991 rang down the curtain on the Soviet Union and its evil empire, liberalism was scoring impressive victories around the world. Let me mention just a few of those gains:

- In December 1978, the Chinese Communist Party began a series of free-market agricultural reforms leading to the most remarkable explosion of farm output in the history of the world.

- On May 3, 1979, Margaret Thatcher won the British General Election and became Prime Minister, promising to dismantle socialism and extend freedom of choice. "The only thing I'm going to do," she pledged, "is make you freer to do things for yourselves. If you can't do it then, I'm sorry, I'll have nothing to offer you."

- On August 30, 1980, 10 million Poles, a third of the population of that country, expressed support for Solidarity, and the Polish Communist Party granted Polish workers the short-lived right to strike.

- On November 4, 1980, the American political establishment was shocked as Ronald Reagan carried all but five states, and Republicans took control of the Senate, gaining 13 seats.

- On October 8, 1982, the reelection of Prime Minister J. R. Jayewardene in Sri Lanka demonstrated that Third World support for the free market wasn't limited to Confucian cultures with authoritarian regimes.

- On November 6, 1982, the selection of Yasuhiro Nakasone as Prime Minister brought to power postwar Japan's most ardent advocate of a strong pro-Western defense, fiscal restraint, and free trade.

- On September 3, 1984, Pope John Paul II condemned Marxist aspects of liberation theology.

- On December 7, 1984, China's *People's Daily* ran a front-page editorial stating that some of Marx's ideas were "no longer suited" to China's problems.

- On March 25, 1985, India's Prime Minister, Rajiv Gandhi, revealed. India's economic potential as tax cuts ignited Bombay's stock market boom.

- During the 1980s, the "Chicago Boys" of Chile brought inflation under control, privatized social security and several major industries, and paved the way for free elections.

- In May 1985, even Tanzania's President, Julius Nyerere, admitted that the nationalization of sisal plantations had destroyed the country's economy.

- Between January and July 1986, the free fall in oil prices—from $26 to $12 a barrel—symbolized the collapse of the OPEC cartel.

- On March 16, 1986, the election of Prime Minister Jacques Chirac in France led to denationalization, lower taxes, and greater freedom for entrepreneurs.

No wonder that, in 1983, the British historian Paul Johnson called the final chapter of his great book, *Modern Times,* "Palimpsests of Freedom." For what this brief survey suggests is that, well before the collapse of the Soviet Empire, statism was already on the ropes everywhere. Whether this proves that Milton was correct when he said that we had essentially won the economic battle back in 1972, or whether it demonstrates that the forces of a resurgent liberalism were immeasurably strengthened after Ed Feulner was elected to membership in the Mont Pelerin Society is a matter I will gladly leave to the historians.

What is unquestionably true, however, is that members of the Mont Pelerin Society have played an important role in this great, global revival of freedom. I need only mention four political names to indicate the scope, range, and depth of the Society's influence: Ludwig Erhard, who, along with fellow liberals from the "Freiburg Circle," laid the foundations for Germany's economic resurgence; Margaret Thatcher, not a member of the Society but a leader who drew heavily from senior members like Arthur Seldon, Ralph Harris, and Peter Bauer in designing her program of reform and drew on our younger members like John O'Sullivan for help in articulating it; Ronald Reagan, also not a member of the Society but a leader who drew on an extraordinarily large number of our members to formulate and implement his programs; and Vaclav Klaus, the first member of our Society in Eastern Europe who today, as Prime Minister of the Czech Republic, presides over his country's transition from communism to capitalism.

Of course, it can always be argued that these individuals would have acted as they did even if the Mont Pelerin Society had never existed. At the very least, however, the experience of discussing common problems with like-minded classical liberals surely strengthened their resolve and relieved their isolation at a time in which liberalism was far from intellectually ascendant.

But what of the situation today? If, in 1889, William Gladstone's Chancellor of the Exchequer, Sir William Harcourt, could say, "We are all socialists now," and if, in 1971, President Nixon could say, "We are all Keynesians now," can it be said in 1997, "We are all liberals now?" I think not. For as James Buchanan wisely observed, "Socialism is dead, but Leviathan lives on."

To be sure, when a dyed-in-the-wool statist like President Bill Clinton is forced to declare that the "era of big government is over," and when Prime Minister Tony Blair, leader of the Labour Party in Great Britain, pledges to continue privatization, it is impossible to deny that something significant is happening. Yet the fact remains that, in the United States, big government has gotten bigger than ever, despite the so-called Conservative Revolution of 1994 that gave Republicans control of the House of Representatives for the first time in 40 years. Every year, U.S. regulators continue to publish another 60,000 pages of new regulations in the *Federal Register.* Our federal government continues to collect $1.6 trillion a year from taxpayers and state and local governments take another trillion, yet the federal deficit continues to grow. Meanwhile, new causes—like environmentalism, health care reform, and others— threaten to expand Leviathan's powers even further.

In part, the reason for big government's continued growth is that, despite their rhetoric, statists like President Clinton and Vice President Al Gore are genuinely wedded to big government, making all their efforts at "reinvention" half-hearted at best. As the Bible puts it, "The voice is Jacob's, but the hands are Esau's." And when Esau tries to wrap his hands around one-seventh of the U.S. economy through health care reform, to subvert property rights through environmental reform, and to undermine the most fundamental social institution—the family—through "family assistance" programs that promote crime, illegitimacy, and sexual promiscuity, liberalism as we understand it cannot be said to have triumphed.

But a deeper problem, I think, is that going from a Western welfare state to a truly free, deregulated society is a transformation almost as great and far-reaching as the transition from communism to capitalism. Consequently, the gulf between winning the battle of ideas and translating those ideas into laws that genuinely diminish Leviathan's power is a very wide one—much wider, perhaps, than we liberals had realized. As Max Hartwell again points out in his splendid *History of the Mont Pelerin Society:*

> In the history of ideas there are identifiable periods in which an idea about how society should be organized is clearly articulated and circulated and acquires legitimacy and acceptance. The idea is then embodied in laws that control and condition the actions of populations.... Rhetoric is not enough. Only when ideas are accepted and also become laws does the world change. Some ideas, even with wide circulation, do not result in changes in policy, or they do so only after a time lag of indefinite length.

In other words, it is possible for us liberals to win the war of ideas but nonetheless to fail to change the world. Ideas are decisive, but not self-implementing; translating even popular ideas into policies and laws capable of reversing 50 years of statist hegemony is not an automatic, straightforward process. In fact, as public choice theory points out, it is made more difficult by the democratic forces freedom-loving peoples fight to preserve.

How, then, do we translate our ideas into laws that not only block the road to serfdom but also clear the path to freedom? Today, this has become a key question. Living in a society in which everyone "naturally" looks to government to solve every problem, how do we return power to the individual? Having been accustomed by the welfare state to think exclusively of their government for security and entitlements, how do we encourage a sense of greater personal responsibility in our fellow citizens? How do we change the current "calculus of consent"?

After decades of relentless attack on such "mediating" institutions as neighborhoods, churches, and voluntary associations, how do we breathe new life into the "little platoons," as Edmund Burke called them, of civil society?

And after the incalculable human suffering caused by government intervention in so many aspects of our lives—especially in the lives of the poor—how do we begin the healing? How do we articulate the very real virtues of the marketplace?

I don't know all the answers to these questions, and perhaps neither do you. I am convinced, however, that, as a group, we must reach beyond the economic realm to the historians and political philosophers Hayek thought were underrepresented at that first meeting and to businessmen, artists, and the religious to build the "critical intellectual mass" to address these questions creatively and constructively and move toward Hayek's goal of articulating a comprehensive "philosophy of freedom."

There is one other world leader who has been profoundly affected by works of our Society's members whom I haven't mentioned yet: Pope John Paul II. (As Professor Rappard feared, I've returned to the Catholics!) As someone who lived much of his life prior to the papacy under communist totalitarianism and someone who has devoted much of his work as Pope to making the *moral* argument for freedom, I think John Paul has provided us with an important vision of our comprehensive philosophy. In his

October 1995 address to the United Nations
General Assembly, titled "The Moral Structure
of Freedom," he said,

> The revolutions of 1989 were made
> possible by the commitment of brave
> men and women inspired by a differ-
> ent, and ultimately more profound and
> powerful, vision: the vision of man as a
> creature of intelligence and free will,
> immersed in a mystery which tran-
> scends his own being and endowed
> with the ability to reflect and the ability
> to choose—and thus capable of wis-
> dom and virtue.

You know, the Keynesian economist and
Nobel Laureate Robert Solow once joked that
the difference between himself and Milton
Friedman was that, to Milton, everything
always comes back to money, whereas to Solow
everything always comes back to sex. I think
that, to all of us here this evening, everything
always comes back to freedom. The issues we
consider are sometimes quite technical—deval-
uation, regionalism and multilateralism in
international trade, the pros and cons of a
return to the gold standard, privatization
schemes, and so forth—but the underlying
theme informing all of our deliberations is an

abiding moral concern for the mind, the soul, and the rights of the individual. That's what unites us. That's the common thread linking us back to our founders and forward to our successors. We are part of an ongoing struggle, and we will continue to insist that families, communities, and individuals—*not* government—have the freedom to make the decisions that shape their lives.

Fifty years after the founding of our Society, we no longer can think of ourselves as a Saving Remnant, huddled together for warmth and encouragement on a dark and stormy night. But neither can we think of ourselves as winners, despite the fact that many of our ideas have gained wide acceptance. In my opinion, we should regard ourselves, first and foremost, as pilgrims, still engaged in the same quest—as individuals and as a society—that inspired our founders: the quest for a comprehensive philosophy of freedom, for a political, social, and economic order that best protects the mind, the soul, and the rights of the individual.

As it happens, the French word for pilgrim is *pelerin.* Perhaps the decision to be known as the Mont Pelerin Society was not quite so meaningless as some of our founders supposed.

In closing, let me once again quote John Paul II—from his closing paragraph of that same speech. His vision is one that I personally share and one that has shaped much of my own life's work.

> We must not be afraid of the future. We must not be afraid of man. It is no accident that we are here. Each and every human person has been created in the "image and likeness" of the One who is the origin of all that is. We have within us the capacities for wisdom and virtue. With these gifts, and with the help of God's grace, we can build in the next century and the next millennium a civilization worthy of the human person, a true culture of freedom. We can and must do so! And in doing so, we shall see that the tears of this century have prepared the ground for a new springtime of the human spirit.

Thank you all for joining us for this special celebration of the anniversary of the Mont Pelerin Society. And a special thank you to Milton Friedman: We all owe a tremendous debt of gratitude to you and the other founders of our Society for making that first pilgrimage to Mont Pelerin 50 years ago.

2

SEVEN PRINCIPLES
OF A FREE SOCIETY

T hank you very much, Mr. Chairman. I well remember the last Spanish Regional Meeting of the Mont Pelerin Society in Madrid, and those who were there will remember, I am sure, the little incident when we took the excursion. An hour and a half into the coach ride, each of us on separate buses looked around and said, "Where is Professor Hayek?" Well, he had failed to awaken that morning in the hotel so we had to call back to the hotel and wake him up, and he came out in a taxi. The reason I recall that incident is that, as Victoria Curzon-

Presidential Address delivered to the 1997 Regional Meeting of the Mont Pelerin Society, September 10, 1997, in Barcelona, Spain.

Price knows well since we were on the bus together, I told her I wanted to make one slight correction to my speech and when I went to pull my speech out, there was no speech. Fortunately, things work very efficiently here in Barcelona with cell phones and what-not, and the speech appeared, so we are now ready for this momentous event—38 pages!

Before I begin, I would like to thank our dear friends from Barcelona who have done such a magnificent job, both in terms of the program itself, which looks to be very stimulating, and also in terms of the organization for this meeting.

So, ladies and gentlemen, dear friends and colleagues in the Society, and my fellow pilgrims:

When we Americans write about Spain, it generally is to contrast its statist traditions with our own liberal traditions, and to demonstrate how the former lead to ruin and the latter to greatness. I am therefore especially grateful to our Society's Treasurer, Professor Leonard Liggio, who in 1990 delivered a paper at our Regional Meeting in Guatemala on "The Hispanic Tradition of Liberty" that presented a very different history of the real Spanish tradition. "During the five hundred years of the *Reconquista,*" Professor Liggio argued,

> the Germanic concepts of law and political institutions flourished in Spain. In the various kingdoms of Spain, the rights of freemen were clearly recognized.... English legal and constitutional history, with the Magna Carta, was parallel to the experiences in Spain, such as the Great Charter of 1020 issued by the Cortes of Leon under Alphonso V.

Leonard convincingly maintained that Spain's medieval history can serve as a source of inspiration for modern liberals, and it is in that spirit—the spirit of intellectual pilgrims earnestly searching for inspiration in our quest for the Promised Land—that I join our Spanish hosts in welcoming you to this meeting of our Society.

I think it is significant for two specific additional reasons that we are meeting in Barcelona. The first is that there have, in fact, been significant constitutional developments. One of these occurred during the Middle Ages, when the Catalonian Kings had to swear allegiance on their coronation to every provision—and, indeed, every letter—of the Constitution. In fact, the oaths were so strong and so mutual that the nobility and gentry owed allegiance to their rulers only if the rulers acted according to the Constitution, and, as the expression goes, "If not, not." This was, of course, an early and important advance to European constitutionalism.

Barcelona was also significant in earlier days because of Consolado de Mar, the law of merchants and seas that evolved originally from Rhodes through Amalfi and which, as two former presidents of this Society, Professors Hayek and Leoni, have pointed out, were important to the evolutionary process of law evolving into the common law.

It is fitting that our meeting here in Barcelona has as its theme "Fifty Years of Liberalism in Europe." The past 50 years of our Society, it seems to me, can be thought of in terms of two quintessentially Spanish figures: Don Quixote, the Knight of the Sorrowful Countenance, and El Cid, the conqueror of Valencia. In the early days, our members must have felt like Don Quixote—engaged in a noble quest—but with the overwhelming majority of Western intellectuals and social scientists opposed to their ideas. They were thought to have as much chance of restoring the principles of classical liberalism as Don Quixote had of reviving the Age of Chivalry in Spain. Yet, today, 50 years after embarking on our "quixotic" quest, liberal arguments for capitalism and against socialism—once bitterly contested—have become the broadly shared assumptions of both the left and the right. I take this incredible transformation of the climate of opinion to be the moral and intellectual equivalent of El Cid's conquest of Valencia.

It is important to remember, however, that El Cid did not complete the reconquest of Spain from the Moors; much hard fighting lay ahead. Similarly, although the welfare state is widely recognized as being in a state of economic and moral crisis, we have not reconquered any significant territory for the principles of liberalism—at least, not yet. Consequently, just as defeating totalitarianism was the great challenge facing our predecessors 50 years ago, so dismantling the welfare state is our great challenge today. As I pointed out in Mont Pelerin, Switzerland, to our Special Gathering just five months ago, "How to translate our ideas into laws that not only block the road to serfdom, but also clear a path to freedom?" has become the key question facing liberals today.

This evening, with your indulgence, I'd like to begin where I left off in April and lay out some of the principles that, in my view, ought to inform the current phase of our struggle. I use the word "principles" advisedly, since to go beyond them and try to draw up a detailed blueprint of the ideal liberal state is to risk falling prey to what Michael Oakeshott calls "Rationalism in Politics," and what Friedrich Hayek referred to as the error of "constructivism."

So, tonight, I will share with you, if I may, seven liberal principles. We as liberals believe in a spontaneous order emerging through the unintended consequences of "human action." Still, there are certain broad principles, attitudes, and predispositions to which most liberal thinkers subscribe, and it is my intention now to discuss these seven. Specifically, I will talk about liberty, competition and free enterprise, heritage, self-government, character, family, and courage. I will not discuss each of them exhaustively, I can assure you.

To begin with the most obvious—and, as George Orwell says, "We have now sunk to a depth at which the restatement of the obvious is the first duty of intelligent men"—we liberals believe in liberty. Of course, statists also purport to believe in liberty, but the nature of those beliefs turns out to be markedly different from ours. Statists invariably distinguish between "human rights," on the one hand, and mere "property rights" on the other. They say they are for the former, but they either disregard, or actively undermine, the latter. And we see this throughout our different societies.

Liberals, on the other hand, believe that economic, social, and political freedom are inseparable—part of the same yearning of the human spirit. Our colleague Milton Friedman is especially eloquent on this point. In his great book, *Capitalism and Freedom*—which, incidentally, will be republished next year—he defends "the fundamental proposition that freedom is one whole, that anything that reduces freedom in one part of our lives is likely to affect freedom in the other parts."

Because we differ so fundamentally over the nature of liberty, it is not surprising that liberals and statists also disagree about the nature of the competitive free enterprise system. Statists regard the free market as a powerful and dangerous enemy that stands in constant need of regulation, supervision, and constraint. We liberals regard it as a major force for good—a force, moreover, that often comes up with unsuspected, creative solutions to pressing social problems.

Support for the free enterprise system based on free and open competition is the second principle I wish to highlight. Far from wishing to constrain free markets, we liberals advocate extending choice and competition to non-market sectors of society—endorsing such measures as privatization to rescue our social security systems, school vouchers to improve our educational systems, and medical savings accounts and patient choice to restructure our health care systems.

"Whenever the free market has been permitted to operate," Milton and Rose Friedman write in their book, *Free to Choose*, "wherever anything approaching freedom of opportunity has existed, the ordinary man has been able to attain levels of living never dreamed of before." Indeed, it is *precisely* because the lives of ordinary men and women have been revolutionized by the free market that liberals cherish it as one of humanity's greatest benefactors and are appalled by statist efforts to undermine it. I hasten to point out that our horror is in no way mitigated by the fact that statists sometimes mean well. Liberals are acutely aware of that "paradox of human nature." The American literary critic Lionel Trilling, a man with whom I don't often agree, once noted that

> the paradox of human nature leads us, once we have made our fellow men the object of our enlightened interest, to go on to make them the objects of our pity, then of our wisdom, ultimately of our coercion.

But there is another paradox of which liberals are keenly aware: the remarkable fact that institutions of such incredible complexity as the free market and the legal structure that makes it possible arose not through deliberate human design but through a spontaneous process of social evolution fueled by the forces of competition. This paradoxical insight was central to the thought of our founder, Friedrich von Hayek, who maintained that the amount of unarticulated knowledge embodied in social processes is far beyond our comprehension, making it impossible for us to engage in deliberate social planning. In his work, *The Constitution of Liberty*, Hayek points out that

> Compared with the totality of knowledge which is continually utilized in the evolution of a dynamic civilization, the difference between the knowledge

that the wisest and that which the most ignorant individual can deliberately employ is comparatively insignificant.

The epistemological modesty so characteristic of Hayek's thought sharply distinguishes us from statists, who rather immodestly assume that if the "Best and Brightest" were running the government, and the government were running us, all would be well. But as we liberals delight in pointing out, governmental interventions in the larger society are not only ineffective, but in case after case they result in the exact opposite of their intended consequence.

I recall Professor Antonio Martino's 1990 presidential address to our Society in which he quoted Alphonso X, the 13th century king of Castile, who said: "If the Lord Almighty had consulted me before embarking on the Creation, I would have recommended something simpler." But because the Lord (alas!) did not see fit to consult me—or, as far as I know, any of us—we choose to place our trust not in our fellow men—limited and fallible as even the best of us are—but rather in free markets, constitutional laws, and inherited traditions.

Because they embody the wisdom and experience of posterity, these institutions are a vital part of our heritage, and it is precisely this heritage that liberals seek to uphold. Professor Irving Kristol has pointed out that liberalism assumes

> that institutions which have existed over a long period of time have a reason and a purpose inherent in them, a collective wisdom incarnate to them, and the fact that we don't perfectly understand or cannot perfectly explain why they work is no defect in them but merely a limitation on us.

Again, this attitude stands in stark contrast to that of the typical statist, who generally regards the institutions bequeathed to us by posterity as guilty until proven innocent.

The liberal's trust in the traditions and institutions of his society leads him to conclude that ordinary citizens, guided by these institutions and traditions, are perfectly capable of governing themselves. He is therefore a champion of popular self-government—the fourth liberal principle—in a way that the statist, convinced that individuals and families stand in constant need of guidance and supervision by experts, is not.

At the same time, the liberal recognizes that if liberty is not to degenerate into license, citizens must be amply endowed with what the American Founders called "republican virtue"—such traits of character as honesty, kindness, thoughtfulness, respect for law, fairness, self-discipline, and self-reliance. Hayek recognizes the welfare state's threat to character when he warns us in *The Road to Serfdom* that the "most important change which extensive government control produces is a psychological change, an alteration in the character of the people." Such character changes—so gradual as to be almost imperceptible—can have huge consequences. "It makes no small difference," said Aristotle, "whether we form habits of one kind or of another from our very youth; it makes a very great difference, or rather, *all* the difference."

Liberals strongly endorse Aristotle's, and Hayek's, emphasis on the importance of good character—so much so, in fact, that support for such character-building institutions as families, neighborhoods, schools, churches and synagogues, Chambers of Commerce, Boy Scouts, and Little Leagues is the fifth principle on my list. These are what Edmund Burke called the "little platoons" that induct the individual into the values and ideals of our larger society.

Of these little platoons, families are especially important. The family, our colleague Michael Novak has pointed out, is the original and most effective Department of Health, Education, and Welfare—the place in which we each receive our first, and most enduring, lessons about faith, education, authority, and civility. Our colleague, Gary Becker, has explored the role of families in creating "human capital"—the knowledge, skills, values, and habits of their children. With the advent of the Information Age, human capital has become increasingly vital to economic growth, and families, as the ultimate seedbeds of human capital, have grown more central than ever. Strengthening the family is my sixth liberal principle.

We believe that strong families, vibrant neighborhoods, thriving communities, multiple levels of self-government, and a society informed by the spirit of competitiveness, free enterprise, and respect for long-standing institutions and traditions are the surest antidotes to what Alexis de Tocqueville singles out as the gravest threat to liberty: that "immense and tutelary power" of the central government, as he puts it in *Democracy in America*, whose

power is absolute, minute, regular, provident and mild. It would be like the authority of a parent if, like that authority, its object was to prepare men for manhood; but it seeks, on the contrary, to keep them in perpetual childhood.

Tocqueville continues,

I have always thought that servitude of the quiet, regular and gentle kind which I have just described might be combined more easily than is commonly believed with some of the outward forms of freedom, and that it might even establish itself under the wing of the sovereignty of the people.

History bears out Tocqueville's fears. That "immense and tutelary power"—that quiet servitude—that he foresaw over 150 years ago we know today as the welfare state. Because its failures, in the words of our colleague Vaclav Klaus, are "less visible, less transparent, less dramatic" than totalitarian forms of statism, they also are more difficult "to see, to understand, [and] to refute." Besides, the welfare state offers the seductive promise of "cradle-to-grave" security—and if, in their passage from cradle to grave, people end up surrendering their freedom to this "quiet, regular, and gentle kind" of servitude, how many will notice, or even bother to pay heed to, prophets like Hayek and their prescient warnings about the road to serfdom?

Fortunately, a few people did pay heed. Along with Hayek, liberals like Ludwig von Mises, Karl Popper, Lionel Robbins, Wilhelm Roepke, Frank Knight, Salvador de Madariaga, and Milton Friedman came together 50 years ago at Mont Pelerin to present an alternative to the statist philosophies that dominated the intellectual landscapes of Europe and the United States. These founders were blessed with what Anatole France called the "rarest courage—the courage of thought."

And, finally, courage may be the most important principle of all, for we all know that it takes courage to challenge popular political and academic leaders when they are wrong; it takes courage to push for reform even when it goes against powerful interests; and it takes courage to spread our ideas where we know they are not welcomed but are needed most.

Today, it is our privilege to stand on the shoulders of our founders and draw on their courage and insights, in addressing a growing public that has become increasingly disillusioned with the fool's gold of statism.

In an address to students at Notre Dame University in 1981, President Ronald Reagan assured his audience that the West would not simply contain communism, it would *transcend* communism. Similarly, we liberals must not be content merely to slow down the rate of big government's growth; we must transcend the welfare state altogether. And we will transcend it, not by placing our hopes in the "human designs" of politicians and experts, but by relying on "human action"—the spontaneous activities of millions of people around the world taking responsibility for their families and neighborhoods, their streets and schools, and their needy, ailing, or troubled fellow citizens—and demonstrating that choice and competition promote human welfare far more effectively than the so-called welfare state can.

In *The Constitution of Liberty*, Friedrich Hayek observes that "Liberty and responsibility are inseparable." Similarly, our friend Charles Murray writes that "Responsibility is not the 'price' of freedom but its reward. Responsibility is what keeps our lives from being trivial." Restoring personal freedom and responsibility is ultimately what the liberal *Reconquista* is all about, and I believe that we can best clear that path to freedom by enabling individuals, families, and private and local institutions to challenge big government in addressing our needs.

The process by which we transcend the welfare state is not a simple one. Furthermore, it will not happen through one mighty burst of legislation or such a dramatic event as the collapse of the Berlin Wall. Instead, it will happen slowly and gradually in one area of civil society after another. I cannot tell you how long it will take, but I can tell you who its heroes will be: They will be the intellectuals with the courage to speak the truth; they will be ordinary people who take responsibility for themselves and their families; they will be religious and community leaders—men and women of character—who are willing to uphold and pass on their faith and heritage; and they will be political leaders who have enough love of freedom, belief in the free enterprise system, and faith in the common man that they, too, are willing to limit the role of the government.

When our struggle is finally won, and the history of our reconquest is written, I believe that the Mont Pelerin Society—this group of courageous men and women—will occupy a place of honor among freedom's staunchest champions and liberalism's most effective leaders.

Thank you.

3

RENEWING THE
FREE SOCIETY

T hank you, my dear friend, Pascal [Salin].
Let me begin by welcoming all of you to
Washington, D.C., a city long known to Americans for its unique blend of Northern charm
and Southern efficiency. It's been said that
Washington is too small to be a state and too
large to be a lunatic asylum. I don't know about
that, but I do know that if I should some day
take leave of my senses entirely, I'd be awfully
lucky to be working in Washington, where no
one would be likely to notice.

Presidential Address delivered to the 1998 General Meeting of the Mont Pelerin Society, August 30, 1998, in
Washington, D.C.

I began my tenure as president of the Mont Pelerin Society with a speech at our special gathering at Mont Pelerin that discussed the ideas of our founding fathers—great intellects like Friedrich von Hayek, Milton Friedman, Wilhelm Roepke, and Karl Popper. Let me now begin this conclusion to my presidency with some reflections on another gifted group of Founding Fathers—George Washington, Thomas Jefferson, George Mason, John Adams, and James Madison—who began a great experiment in limited government over 200 years ago, one that continues to inspire all of us in the Mont Pelerin Society today.

It is sometimes said that, unlike their wild-eyed, utopian-minded, ideology-driven French counterparts, the authors of the American Revolution were sober, serious, practical statesmen. There is surely much truth in this contention, but I fear that it threatens to obscure a more important truth: The American Founders were *revolutionaries,* profoundly convinced that they were inaugurating a "new order for the ages." They were indeed sober and serious when designing a representative form of government because they entertained a healthy skepticism toward all forms of centralized state power and a well-founded suspicion that, unless its authority were strictly limited, government would soon envelop the whole of society in its suffocating embrace.

But if the Founding Fathers deeply distrusted *public* man, they had an abiding faith in the capacities of *private* man, working with his friends, his neighbors and his community to build a just, decent, and free society. As Thomas Jefferson, after enumerating America's many blessings, put it in his first Inaugural Address,

> Still one thing more, fellow citizens—a wise and frugal government, which shall restrain men from injuring one another, which shall leave them otherwise free to regulate their own pursuits of industry and improvement, and shall not take from the mouth of labor the bread it has earned. This is the sum of good government.

For the first 150 years of America's existence, this Jeffersonian vision of limited government maintained its hold on the American imagination. But with the onset of Progressivism and the New Deal, many Americans became attracted to a political philosophy that was diametrically opposed to Jefferson's. This new statist philosophy had great faith in *public* man, but was deeply distrustful of *private* man. It maintained, quite incorrectly, that the uncoordinated activities of ordinary individuals were bound to culminate in economic catastrophes like the Great Depression, and it looked to an all-good, all-wise, and increasingly all-powerful central government to set things right. In the view of these statists—who brazenly hijacked the term *liberal* to describe their very illiberal philosophy—what we Americans needed was more government, not less.

Of course, it was not only, or even primarily, in the United States that this pernicious statism took hold. Everywhere, it seemed, statism was the wave of the future, and the 39 men and women who founded our Society in 1947 appeared to be engaged in a hopeless undertaking: the revival of classical liberalism in a world whose growing complexity supposedly required that individual freedom be ever-more sharply curtailed.

As we all know, however, events have vindicated the vision of our Society's founders. Today, statism is widely discredited and big government is increasingly recognized as the problem, not the solution. As far as the American experience is concerned, two revealing pieces of polling data say it all: In 1964, when President Lyndon Johnson embarked on that vast expansion of federal power known as the

"Great Society," 75 percent of all Americans said that they trusted the federal government. Today, responding to an identical question, 75 percent of all Americans declare that they do *not* trust the federal government. Once hailed as the "wave of the future," big government is now more accurately perceived as the dead hand of the past.

But although the welfare state has lost even its appearance of moral legitimacy and no longer enjoys what traditional Chinese would call the "Mandate of Heaven," the disquieting fact remains that it is still in place, still metastasizing, still blighting the lives of millions and millions of ordinary citizens. As one of our founders, Milton Friedman, wrote in his welcoming remarks, today "there is less talk of socialism, yet governments are bigger and more intrusive."

How is that possible? How can it be that in democratic societies based on majority rule, the barriers to free markets and free people are still largely intact?

One powerful answer to this question is provided by public choice theory—an insight into social, economic, and political processes pioneered by our Mont Pelerin Society members James Buchanan and Gordon Tullock. As public choice theorists see it, an "Iron Triangle" of bureaucrats, politicians, and special interests often can block change, thwart the popular will, and manipulate public policy in favor of the status quo. In the case of the welfare state, the power of this Iron Triangle is significantly augmented by a "New Class" of intellectuals, who derive much of their status from their association with big government and who can be counted on to buttress the eroding moral foundations of the welfare state with a whole host of specious arguments.

I think public choice theory explains a lot, but I would like to offer an additional reason for the persistence of statist barriers to freedom in an anti-statist age. When I compare current with traditional American attitudes toward state and society, it strikes me that, although both the American Founders and contemporary Americans distrust public man, they have strikingly different attitudes toward private man. As I already noted, the Founders had a burning faith in the ability of ordinary people to accomplish extraordinary things once they were freed from the fetters of big government. But modern Americans, who grew up in a welfare state and became accustomed to delegating so many of life's tasks to a gigantic bureaucracy, simply aren't sure that they can take up the slack on their own. In the absence of big government, they ask, who would help the poor? Who would protect the environment? Who would see to the educational needs of our children? Who would guarantee an adequate level of health care? Who would provide a decent living for the old, the sick, and the disadvantaged? Who, in short, would serve as his brother's keeper—if not Big Brother himself?

When I consider the attitudes of Americans toward big government today, I am irresistibly reminded of Poland in the late 1970s. Back then, Poles had lost all confidence in the moral pretensions of their communist government. Back then, an Iron Triangle consisting of the Communist Party, the security services, and the armed might of the Soviet Union effectively guaranteed the status quo. And back then, while ordinary Poles rejected the status quo, they simply lacked the confidence to imagine that private individuals, voluntarily cooperating with other private individuals, could mount an effective challenge to the seemingly overwhelming power of the Polish state.

But then, in 1979, something remarkable happened: Pope John Paul II, the first Pole ever to occupy St. Peter's throne, spent nine days visit-

Pope's pilgrimage was overwhelming. Day after day, literally millions of Poles gathered to hear the Pope's words, and while these words were by no means inflammatory or provocative, the mere presence of so many people acting on their own, in defense of deeply held religious values, suddenly filled Polish society with a new sense of self-confidence. Out of this self-confidence came the trade union known as Solidarity, and 10 years after Solidarity's formation, the "Evil Empire" was finished.

It seems to me that we liberals today must try to accomplish in our own societies what the Pope achieved in Poland: to awaken—or, rather, to reawaken—a sense of the power, ingenuity, and creativity of civil society. We need to convince our fellow citizens that the tasks the public sector performs so poorly today could be performed far better by the private sector tomorrow. We need to demonstrate that there are more compassionate ways of helping the poor; more enlightened ways of protecting the environment; more effective ways of educating our children, healing our sick, and tending to our elderly than to rely on the "invisible foot" of a distant bureaucracy.

To achieve such a renewal of civic confidence, we cannot use blueprints drawn up by the founders of the Mont Pelerin Society—for the simple reason that our founders never prepared any such blueprints. On the contrary, they specifically warned us against what Hayek called "constructivism"—the error of assuming that centralized planning somehow can improve on the spontaneous, uncoordinated activities of free human beings.

But if we are lacking in blueprints, surely we are not lacking in brains—or in boldness, or in the capacity to help to foster a creative climate of economic, social, and political innovation. Around the world, remarkable innovations in public policy are taking place, and many of our members are in the thick of the action. Our gatherings have always been the occasion in which we, the energizers of a free society, are ourselves re-energized. And perhaps there is no better way to rekindle such a regeneration than to reflect on the impressive body of experience with free markets and free people that we have *already* accumulated.

Let me explain what I mean with a personal example. In the United States, our Social Security system is in serious trouble. Payroll taxes have increased 17 times in the past 40 years, yet promised benefits exceed projected revenues by trillions of dollars. Nonetheless, through very

clever demagoguery, statists have so far succeeded in blocking serious reform. All this
distresses me deeply and, in my despair, I
sometimes imagine that in another five years or
so, the United States and Cuba will be the only
countries in the Western Hemisphere that have
not privatized their retirement systems.

But then I go to Mont Pelerin Society confer-
ences and meet social innovators like José
Piñera, who, as Minister of Labor and Social
Security in Chile, was responsible for the privatization of the Chilean pension system in 1980. I
still recall the brilliant paper José presented to
our Society in January 1996 in Cancun, Mexico,
which described how Chile's privately admin-
istered, national system of Pension Savings
Accounts revitalized the Chilean economy and
empowered Chile's workers. And I say to
myself, "Don't lose hope, Feulner. After all, not
all of the University of Chicago's brightest economics graduates were Chileans!"

But it is not only meetings with Chileans that
re-energize me. In 1986, the left-of-center Labor
government in Australia began to implement
an innovative retirement system based primarily on mandatory private savings in plans
called "superannuation funds." These reforms
are of particular interest to me because Austra-

lia and the United States are similar in many respects. Both are high-income, developed countries with stable democratic governments. In Australia, 11.9 percent of the population is 65 or older, compared with 12.7 percent in the United States. General government outlays in 1996 were 36.9 percent of gross domestic product in Australia and 35.8 percent in the United States. It stands to reason, therefore, that American reformers can learn a lot from the Australian experience, and in meetings with our Australian colleagues like Greg Lindsay, I do everything I can to pick their brains and also to draw them out on both the similarities and the differences between the Australian and Chilean plans.

Of course, picking my colleagues' brains means learning from their mistakes as well as their successes. In recent weeks, Social Security privatization in Great Britain has come under fire because of inadequate consumer protection of workers moving from company plans to private plans. The lesson here is that reformers must be very careful to make sure that workers and retirees are protected against fraud and the abuse and mismanagement of private pension funds—but without falling into the trap of over-regulation.

In my own public policy work here in Washington, I try to apply the lessons I've learned at Mont Pelerin gatherings. In my speaking engagements, my writing, and my meetings with government officials and private citizens, I always emphasize that the privatization of Social Security is not some harebrained scheme devised by ivory-tower economists with no experience of the real world. Instead, it's a tried, tested, and increasingly popular solution to what José Piñera has rightly called a "specter [that] is haunting the world—the specter of a bankrupt pension system."

In one form or another, privatized retirement systems have been adopted in Chile, Australia, Great Britain, Peru, Argentina, Colombia, Mexico, Bolivia, El Salvador, Uruguay, Singapore, Malaysia, Indonesia, Thailand, Hong Kong, Switzerland, Poland, Hungary, Kazakhstan, Slovenia, Denmark, Finland, Sweden, Latvia, the Czech Republic, and Croatia. These privatizations make it clear—not just in theory, but in actual practice—that we don't need Big Brother to look after us in our old age, that we'd be far better off, in fact, if Big Brother simply minded his own business.

Similarly, the educational reforms that have been adopted in various parts of the world demonstrate that Big Brother isn't needed in the classroom, either. As documented in a forthcoming book by Professor Charles Glenn, governments across the world have realized that public funding of elementary and secondary education does not require government control of the schools themselves. Glenn says that most countries in the Organisation for Economic Co-operation and Development—again, my own United States is a glaring exception—provide some sort of public funding for private schools. In most cases, unfortunately, the funds go directly to schools instead of to parents, so there is still a great deal for these countries to learn from Milton Friedman's 36-year-old proposal for vouchers. In addition, there is a real danger that the regulation accompanying government funding will damage the distinctiveness and creativity of the private schools.

But I suspect that scholars and reformers in the United States have a great deal to learn from such experiments as the one taking place in the Netherlands, in which 70 percent of school children attend Dutch Reformed, Roman Catholic, Muslim, Hindu, and other private schools that are funded publicly and three provisions of the Constitution protect the independence of these private schools. I also suspect that non-American educators can learn

a lot from experiments in school choice sweep-
ing the United States—many of which are
privately funded by organizations like the Milton and Rose Friedman Foundation.

I've cited these examples—many, if not all, of
which surely are quite familiar to you—in order
to make a larger point: We are living in the
midst of one of the great creative eras in economic and political history. This is a time in
which brilliant social innovators are applying
the timeless insights of liberalism to expand the
boundaries of personal freedom. And, in contrast with our Society's founders, who could
mount only a theoretical argument against statism, we have a significant body of practical
experience on which to draw. For the past 50
years, we have witnessed countless efforts by
the state to create a host of alphabet-soup agen-
cies to replace the free market. The result of all
these misguided experiments is that, today, you
don't have to be a Nobel Laureate to understand that statism doesn't work. On the
contrary, everyone with eyes with which to see
and a brain with which to think—yes, *everyone*
knows simply by looking around—that the
welfare state does not provide for the welfare of
its citizens. The emperor has no clothes!

Because all of us here today stand on the shoulders of those who preceded us—on freedom-loving statesmen like Jefferson, Madison, Washington, Adams, and Mason—but also on those of a line of great economists stretching back to Adam Smith and including such modern-day giants as Hayek, Roepke, Friedman, Buchanan, Becker, Coase, and Stigler, we can see beyond the moribund welfare state to the free society that, even now, is beginning to replace it. It will be a society firmly based on what Edmund Burke called the "little platoons" of family and school, church, and neighborhood instead of on the cumbersome bureaucracy of the "nanny state." It will be a genuinely compassionate society in which people look after the welfare of the neediest members of their community because they recognize a moral obligation to do so—and not because the state forces them to pay for social programs that end up doing more harm than good. Above all, it will be a society that recognizes that our most precious resource is the human spirit, and that a spirit of creativity and enterprise can flourish only in a climate of freedom.

Renewing the free society through both theory *and* practice is the urgent task of the moment. Provided that we perform this task dutifully, intelligently, and enthusiastically, I am convinced that the upsurge of freedom foreseen by our Society's founders 50 years ago will acquire an irresistible momentum; that civil society will regain the confidence it needs to challenge the "tyranny of the status quo"; that the Iron Triangle's stranglehold will be broken; that the New Class will go the way of the old *nomenklatura;* and that the 21st century will witness a new birth of freedom in Europe, Asia, Africa, Latin America, and even, hopefully, in Washington, D.C.

Thank you one and all for your kindness and your patience, and for making my presidency one of the real highlights of my life. And, once again, welcome to Washington.